THE CASTLE THAT VANISHED

Myths, Mystery – and History

Mary Adams

With the exception of the Appendix, this text was originally published
by
Kent Archaeological Society
as an eBook
on
www.kentarchaeology.ac

Illustrations: – Author's Own Photographs and Maps

Published by Mary Adams
Mizar, High Halden, Ashford, Kent, England
ISBN

CONTENTS

ACKNOWLEDGMENTS

I am eternally grateful to Dr Michael Stansfield for introducing me to the Christ Church Priory bedel rolls and for his help in discovering how to read them.

I would like to thank Terry Lawson once more for his seemingly unending patience and kindness, and Denis Anstey for his practical help

Philippa Kenyon-Slaney has given me much appreciated help by reading and rereading my script and correcting so many mistakes. Any that remain are 'all my own work'.

I am grateful to the National Trust in the person of Paul Meredith who has given me permission to use the builder's sketch of Ellen Terry's lamp room and to the owners of Horne's Place and Harven who have permitted me, in years gone by, to take photographs in their property.

And special thanks to Dr David Starkey who has supplied photocopies, information and encouragement with incredible kindness and generosity for many years.

MYTHS, MYSTERY AND HISTORY

An Introduction

When I was seventeen I said that I wanted to be an architect. I had become fascinated with buildings when I was about ten, firstly by our village tithe barn which my friend and I trotted off to gaze at after a wireless lesson on tithe barns and later when my mother took out a building licence to build her own bungalow. (Well, actually sub-contractors did the work with me as an enthusiastic labourer until told to run off and play.) However I was told very firmly by my head mistress that there was no future for girls in architecture, the sensible thing was to go off and teach maths and science. And in those far-off days one was sensible!

The result was a life in a lab and spare time spent looking at any sort of building available. It was when the lab days were behind me that I encountered my most important building – the chapel at Horne's Place in Appledore.

The chapel, built of stone, is high, wide and handsome with a cellar underneath and three enormous arched windows. But it has something even more important – a licence issued to William Horne who was living at Horne's Place in 1366. Historians dote on dated documents and local histories all said confidently that, because of the licence, there was no doubt that the chapel was built in 1366. Well – some said soon after 1366 because windows like those in the chapel weren't being made much before 1400. In fact having these windows made the chapel even more remarkable.

The trouble was that the chapel didn't look so much like a chapel as a conversion job. The huge east window, because of the way it was set into the surrounding stonework,

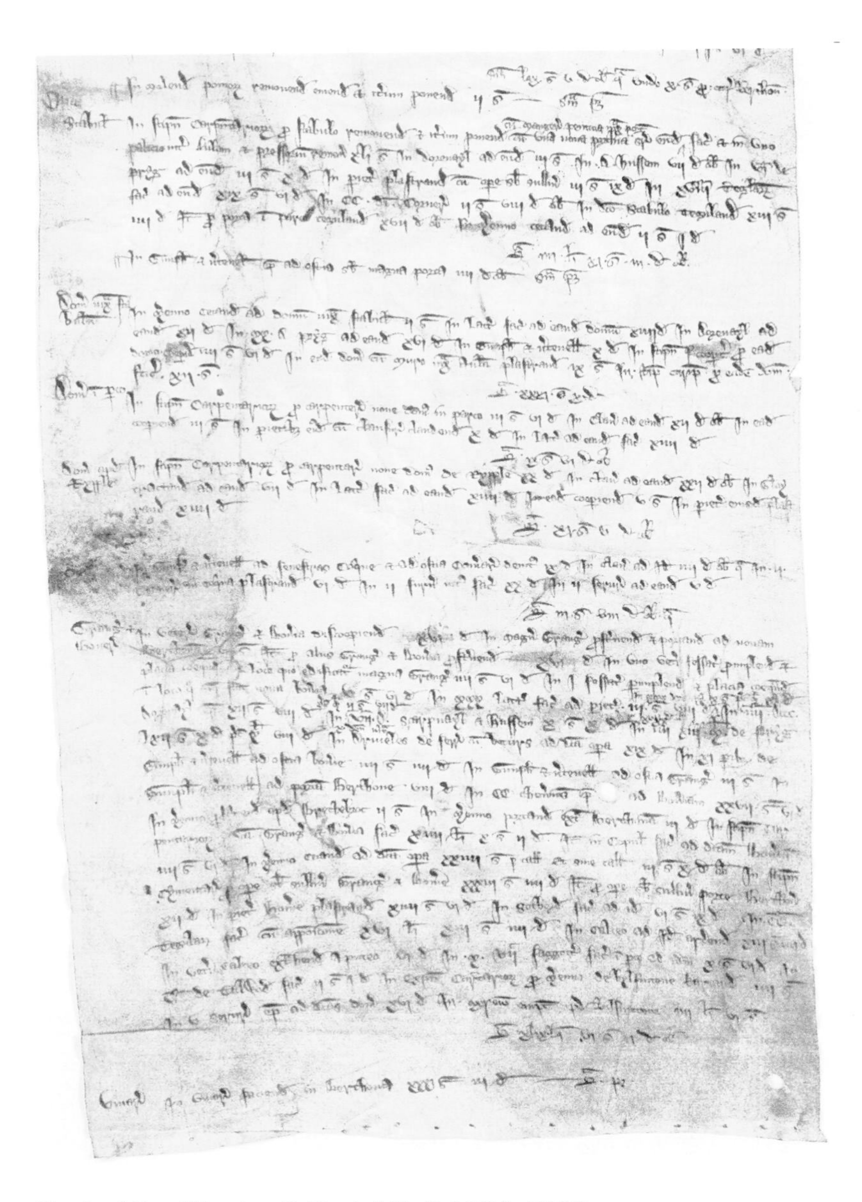

Part of the Westwell Bedel Roll 1291-1292

was obviously a replacement, and much of the rest of the building seemed to have been knocked down and rebuilt.

'These were', said the historians, 'alterations that had taken place when the chapel had been used as a farm building' – but as a farmer's daughter I knew that you didn't spend huge sums of money on dolling up a cowshed for Daisy. I wanted to have a look at that licence.

It turned out that Lambeth Palace held the licence and they were kind enough to send me a copy. Dated November 1366, it said that William Horne might hear Mass in the chapel belonging to his house (not to him) from that date for the period of one year, that is from November 1366 until November 1367. Then it expired. It had nothing to do with building the place.

That is when I went to Canterbury and was first introduced to the building records in the 'Bedel Rolls', balance sheets kept by the monks of Christ Church Priory who farmed at Appledore until the dissolution of the monasteries.

* * * * *

History – Unlocking the Past

History is about people, the places where they lived, what they got up to and the events that influenced their lives. If these were important or interesting enough someone would write about them and where these writings have survived they are gloated over by historians who just love written evidence. There is nothing wrong with this, although perhaps we should remember that we tend not to credit today's newspapers with complete accuracy and perfect truth and it is a good idea to treat earlier writings with the same caution.

It is a different scenario when we come to ordinary people living out their lives in little villages long ago. Not a lot has been written about them and so documents like these bedel rolls, although only designed so that Christ Church Priory could keep tabs on the money due to it, can still yield useful facts. Dating from the end of the thirteenth century into the fifteenth century, they record expenses and income acquired by the priory manors at the time when the events that are responsible for these matters are actually taking place. If you analyse the building expenses they reveal a surprising amount of information about the manors. When you add in the topography of the area, the setting and structure of local buildings and such evidence as is available from wills, inventories and leases, it is possible to put all this evidence together and to formulate a hypothesis about the early development of the area and, to a certain extent, the life of the community there.

However, the amount of documentary evidence from this period is limited; buildings have disappeared or been altered beyond recognition, hedges and field boundaries have changed, manor accounts have been lost and such wills and inventories as survive are those of the better-off members of society. Clearly such a hypothesis is neither complete nor accurate and leaves many questions unanswered about the ordinary people who lived there. Nevertheless for such an area, a village for example, it will present a snapshot, faint and out of focus maybe, but revealing a real community and - more important - it leaves a way open for it to be clarified when more evidence is acquired.

The building up of hypotheses and their later modification is the foundation of much scientific understanding and was something I was forever attempting to teach during all those years in the school lab. John Tosh writing in *The Pursuit of History* about the dialogue between science and history quotes the philosopher of science, Karl Popper, who says: 'scientific knowledge consists not of laws but of the best available hypotheses' and 'because hypotheses go beyond the evidence they necessarily involve - - an imaginative leap'. Tosh goes on to say 'far greater play is allowed to the imagination in history' since historians seek to reconstruct or re-create the past. (In fact you need quite a lot of imagination if you are really to understand – say – the Kinetic Theory of Gases!) Returning to history, certainly imagination is needed to build the hard facts obtained from primary sources into a coherent picture, but because this is a theoretical picture it always has to carry a disclaimer to the end that it is only a 'likely', a 'probably' or an 'almost certainly ' true representation of the past.

Theory precludes certainty. And this is good. The past is a country that we cannot visit populated by a people that we cannot meet. We should not presume on our acquaintance with them.

Since hypothesis is more familiar as a scientific discipline, for many writers the 'accepted facts' obtained from the works of earlier historians are preferable because their long existence seems to guarantee their truth. However, these facts were often propounded before modern investigative methods were available. The modern advances in archaeology have immensely increased our knowledge of the past. Carbon dating, dendro-chronology and Cecil Hewett's pioneering work on medieval carpentry have led to a better understanding of vernacular architecture and so, in understanding more of the work done by our 'rude forefathers' it is possible to learn more about the workmen themselves. In fact the writings of the topographers and antiquarians may well be dangerously flawed and further from the truth than a modern theory with its more modest claims.

I, therefore, make no excuse for the use of hypothesis and the necessary 'imaginative leap' in pursuing the myths and mysteries of the following pages.

* * * * *

Myths

'History is not what you thought. It is what you can remember. All other history defeats itself'. This outrageous view of history expressed in *1066 And all that* by our favourite historians, Sellar and Yeatman, explains, with totally unexpected wisdom, the existence of myths and legends. For that is what they are – the history that has been remembered. The trouble with memories is that Joe Bloggs, as he thinks about the past, always sees events taking place in the world with which he is familiar.

I remember on a family outing turning off a main road and driving a couple of miles down an almost unmetalled lane to visit a cousin who lived in a fifteenth century half-timbered farmhouse. My father, disgusted with having to drive so far along the potholed lane, said that he could not understand why anyone wanted to build a house so far from the main road. It was pointed out to him that when the house was built there was no 'main road' and the decrepit lane was as much a highway as our modern 'A' road. It didn't actually comfort him a lot!

So in the past as Old Joe has passed on to Young Joe the story of some great event, young Joe looking around him has imagined the event taking place amongst the buildings and countryside and fashions that he knows. In turn he has passed on to Little Jo a rather different story from that known to Old Joe. And so on and so on, the story evolving until Old Joe would scarcely have recognised it. Historians with high academic ideals may like to dismiss legends and myths as fairytales – but it may not be a good idea to spurn the memories of the Bloggs family in this high-handed way! There must usually be a reason for them to survive. Therefore, when looking for sources of information, a local myth or legend should never be totally discounted. Distorted and flawed it may be but the possibility that it contains a golden grain of truth is worthy of investigation.

* * * * *

APPLEDORE

The Castle that Vanished

The Appledore Myth is reported with sundry variations by a number of topographers. Kilburne's *Topography* and Thomas Phillipott's *Kent Surveyed*, both published in 1659, give slightly different versions of what is essentially the same story, namely that a Danish castle had survived and that it was included in the 'castles and fortresses of this country until 1380 when the French raid reduced it to a heap of flame and ruin out of whose dismantled reliques the church now visible was not only repaired but, as some from ancient tradition affirm, wholly re-edified'. Charles Seymour's *Survey of Kent* in 1776 adds the observation that the Danish castle was deemed one of the strongest fortresses in this country 'as appears by the Register, till the French demolished it', and Hasted mentions the Myth in 1798. Now, unless these distinguished gentlemen invented the whole thing, it must have originated somewhere.

Later writers, evidently impressed by a myth with such an estimable pedigree, have also quoted it, cheerfully ignoring the fact, acknowledged by Sir John Winifrith in his *History of Appledore,* that the architecture of Appledore church shows that 'the north chapel, the chancel , the arches of the nave and tower were built well over a century before 1380'. Sir John divides the myth into two parts: first, the myth of the stone castle and second, that of the church built from its ruins in 1380, and says that both of them 'are, I believe, without foundation'.

Now, we can either believe that Kilburne and Phillipott in some kind of unholy alliance sat down together and made up the whole story, or we can assume that it must have come about because at some time someone, somewhere, remembered a castle in Appledore.

We are told two things about the castle: that it was knocked down or burnt and that it was built by the Danes.

It is surely impossible that even the Bloggs family memory could stretch back as far as the coming of the Danes. It is the Anglo-Saxon Chronicle that records a Danish invasion in 892 when 250 ships came to the Lympne, rowed four miles upriver and broke into a half built fort occupied by a few peasants. 'Soon after that came Haesten with 80 ships - -. He built himself a fort at Milton Royal, and the other force at Appledore'.

Appledore, between the oak forest with its clay soil to the north and the marsh to the south, was not an area where building stone was plentiful. The nature of the half-built fort, whether the invaders completed it or built one from scratch, we shall probably never know but it seems likely that the Danes got busy with spades and axes and put up an earthwork topped by a timber palisade. Nearly 800 years later it is doubtful whether what was left of this construction would have been recognised as a castle by the local inhabitants. Furthermore, if our information about schooling in the early modern period is correct, these good folk were not much given to curling up by the fire in the evening with a good book and would have lived in blissful ignorance of the Anglo-Saxon Chronicle. It is probable that the 'Danish' input came from educated gentlemen interested in matters historical who would have read about Haesten's invasion.

The knocking down or burning of the castle is rather different, for if our Joe remembered the castle then it is quite possible that he would remember its destruction. Castles were built and then slighted with almost equal enthusiasm but this did not lead to their complete disappearance. There should still be some signs of it in the surrounding countryside and so it would seem to be a good idea to take a look for it there. Thanks to the bedel rolls it is also possible to have some

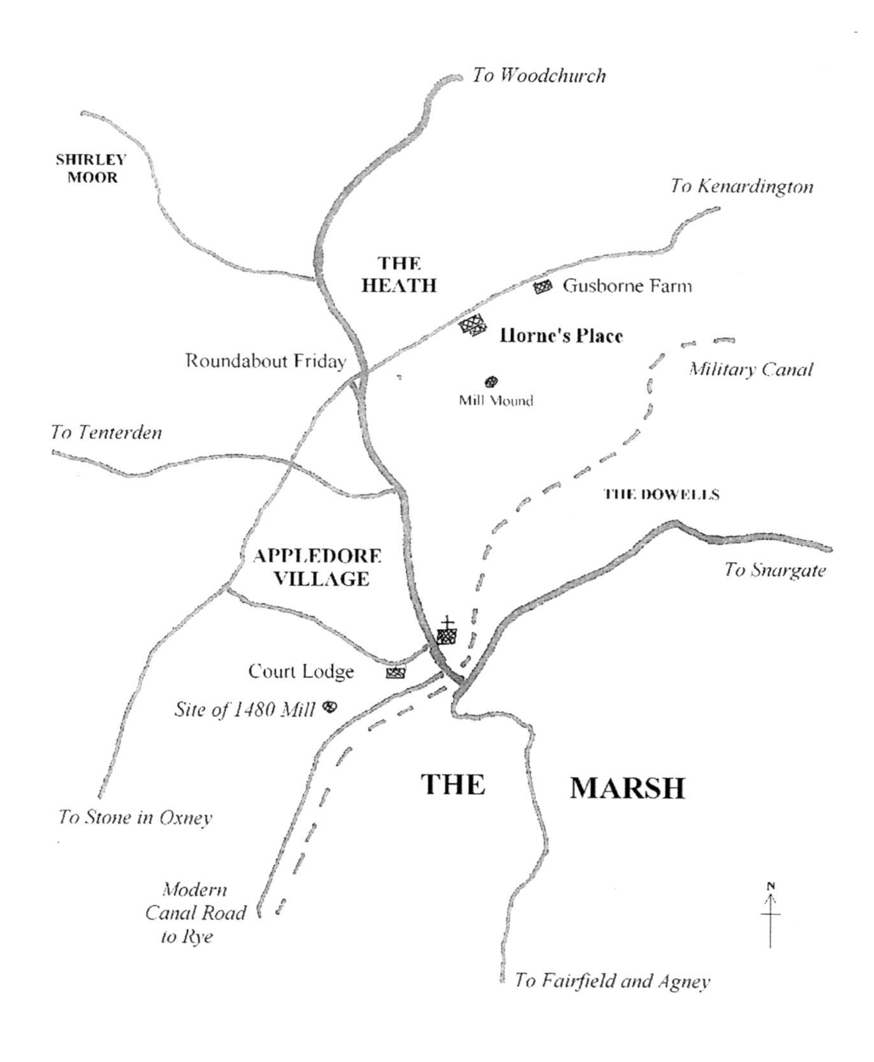

Sketch Map of Part of Appledore Today

notion of what was going on in the locality in the fourteenth century when our fairy-tale castle would still have been in existence.

First of all, south of the village is the Walland Marsh, reclaimed marsh land, with no building other than those belonging to a modern farm to be seen anywhere nearby. Leaving the Marsh, crossing over the Military Canal and moving up the road to the village we come to the village street. On the right is the church. This belonged to Dover Priory (as did some of the land in the parish) and, as Sir John Winnifrith has pointed out, it was certainly not rebuilt from the destroyed castle.

Appledore Church

Opposite to the church is a lane which leads past Court Lodge where once the manor courts were held, the most important house in the village. Today a drive from the entrance leads up to a Victorian villa near to a great manorial barn. This was once the Christ Church Priory demesne farm, sometimes called the barton, sometimes the manor, and from the bedel rolls we know that it was set up on this site just after 1376. At this time, as well as being the Court House, it was also home to the 'farmer' who was renting the manor. The first building erected was a barn which came from Agney where it was taken down and then rebuilt here. In 1379 work started on a timber-framed cross wing house. First of all a chamber and granary, which would have been a store room underneath the chamber, were built, and then a separate timber-framed hall was constructed. Finally an external kitchen was provided. Since the farmer renting the place was a layman no private chapel was provided for his benefit. Many years later this house burnt down, a second one was built and this in turn was replaced by the existing villa. Looking round the site as it is today it is quite clear that there was a large *curia* or farmyard near the house but there is nothing that could be interpreted as the remains of a castle.

The bedel rolls list the income and expenses of the demesne farm from the thirteenth century, so that there must have been a previous farmstead but obviously on a different site. In fact the rolls tell us quite a lot about this earlier manor. The farm was managed by a layman called the serjeant, was supervised by monk wardens who rode down from Canterbury twice a year to check up on things, and was served by the bedel who collected rents and kept the accounts. The priory was notoriously tight-fisted and demanded to know exactly how every farthing was spent, and so the buildings on which work was done are listed as well as the cash. It becomes obvious that this early farm was a pretty impressive place with great barns and stables and cowsheds. There was an *aule* or hall, a prior's chamber, which would have been an upper room, another chamber, an external kitchen and a chapel. The whole complex was entered through a 'great gate'

Now timber structures, roofs and lath and plaster walls needed a good deal of upkeep but over a period of many years there is no mention of any repair to the walls of the hall. In fact it was not until some time after the Black Death that some 'holes' in the walls needed filling. The fact that it needed so little in the way of maintenance suggests that it was built of stone rather than timber. In 1352 it was re-roofed with 50 pairs of 'poles', that is – rafters. Smarden church was built at around this time and its nave boasts a similar number of rafters suggesting that the Appledore *aule* was about the same length, some 27 metres long. At this date the living quarters may have been on the first floor with storage underneath. It must in any case have been a tall and most impressive building. Like the mythical castle, it seems unlikely that it would have disappeared without trace, and since it has a documented history it is something that it should be possible to trace.

Coming back to the village we find records which show that In 1480 John Stylle, a mill-wright, built a windmill on high land just to the west of Court Lodge. This land, now called Mill Hill, bears a striking resemblance to a large earthwork especially when seen from the Canal road as you approach Appledore from Rye. Although it is most probably a purely natural feature and may, of course, have been altered when the military Canal was built, it does stand close to the original channel of the river and it is tempting to wonder if this could be the remains of Haesten's famous fort. In any case, this is certainly not the castle for which we are hunting!

Beyond this point the Court Lodge lane drops away into low ground and the ferry leading to Oxney. No castle here.

Returning to the village street we learn from the bedel rolls that the land to the west of the church was where Christ

Western Escarpment of Mill Hill from the Canal Road

Church Priory rented out a number of shops and stalls. In 1279 there were four shops with counters, a shop close to the church and four stalls, producing 13s a year in rents. By 1297 there were seven shops and five stalls and by 1347 the rent had risen to 18s per annum which was paid half-yearly. However, in 1349 the bedel writes: 'Nine shillings received from the shops in the town and no more because all the holders who used to be there are dead'. The Black Death had come to the town of Appledore.

To the east of the church the ground falls away again into the marsh and the swampy area called the Dowles and there is nothing to suggest that there was ever a castle in this region.

The highway runs northwards from the village street up to a crossroads in the middle of Appledore Heath. Cottages from the eighteenth, nineteenth and twentieth centuries are dotted here and there along the road sides. The highway continues north past little fields with hedges, which are exactly where hedges are shown on a map of 1628, and leads over a hill into Woodchurch. The western branch of the crossroads goes off towards Oxney, the eastern road leads to Warehorne past Horne's Place with its stone built chapel, and this is really the only site which we have found that has obviously been occupied for centuries.

Horne's Place from the Road

Forgetting for the moment the mythical castle and concentrating on the early demesne farm, which had a proven existence, it is tempting to think that we have found it. But it is so easy to jump to wrong conclusions and there are questions that need an answer before we can say that Horne's Place was the original demesne farm.

The first question is: is this site early enough? The bedel roll accounts date back to the latter part of the thirteenth century, so the farm was in existence then. Today a fifteenth century timber-framed house with extravagantly moulded internal timbers showing the enormous wealth and high status of the builder abuts directly on to the north side of the stone chapel. This has long been erroneously dated to around 1366 by the William Horne licence and therefore not much stylistic dating has been undertaken. Stone buildings are not easy to date and window mouldings are a feature commonly used. In this case the windows are in the perpendicular style associated with the fifteenth century, but since examination of the surrounding stonework, particularly in the case of the great east window, shows that they are replacement windows this does not tell us when the walls were built. There are two clues to this. One is the use in the fabric of black, ferruginously-cemented blocks sometimes called iron-ore pudding stones, which are found only in early buildings. The other is the outward appearance of the south-west corner of the chapel, for this is not really a corner at all but a stone rebate combined with a mass of broken masonry. This is best explained as the point where another stone building had once been joined to the corner of the chapel, a not uncommon early building practice. For example, at Plaxtol the thirteenth century stone-built solar of Old Soar Manor is built with both its chapel and its wardrobe (or garde-robe) linked to the corners of the living room. Because this method of construction was short lived it does suggest an early, possibly thirteenth century date, for the chapel at Hornes Place so, if these conclusions are valid, the stone chapel would have been standing when the bedel rolls were written.

The second question is perhaps more pertinent. Since we know William Horne was at Horne's Place from 1366 onwards and that the demesne farm did not leave its original site and move to Court Lodge until around 1379 where was it in the meantime? Does this mean that its original site was elsewhere?

The clue to what happened appears to lie in the terms of that famous licence which permitted William to hear mass in the Horne's Place chapel for just one year.

Prior to Henry VIII's interference parish churches in England owed allegiance to the Pope who responded by taxing them heavily. The king also saw them as a prime source of income with the result that they needed a lot of money to pay their dues and no amount of bullying could obtain this from the peasantry. It was the wealthy who had to be coerced into going to church. They were quite welcome to have private chapels where the monk that they employed to keep their accounts, monks being the men educated to do that sort of thing, could say his daily offices, but the owner was not allowed to celebrate mass in his own oratory. Only in the case of special need was a licence issued which permitted this celebration to take place and it specified exactly when and exactly who could attend. It was an important legal document – the driving licence of its day. The fact that William Horne's licence was for just November 1366 to November 1367 shows that something in which he was playing a part must have been going on during that time.

The bedel rolls for this period tell us exactly what was going on – a new house was being built on the demesne farm and was being put up in a hurry. We know this because it was not being made with newly cut oak in the way the new Court Lodge house was later constructed, a long process, but with the ready made frame of an unwanted old house at Great Chart which was bought for 40 shillings. It was brought to Appledore and re-built. The rolls record the purchase of 800 Flanders tiles for a fireback and hearth where the cooking would have been done. Details of the construction show that it was quite a large building; its roof was covered with 10,500 tiles, and when the restoration was complete it was plastered and lime washed. Although it is described in the rolls as a *coquinna* or kitchen it was obviously quite a fine building capable of providing both bed and board.

So why did the demesne farm want a second house or kitchen on the site where it was already well provided with both? It was certainly not to accommodate a growing work force for at this time the priory was renting out more and more land and farming fewer acres itself. Serfdom was never common in Kent and work on the manor was done mainly by the *famuli* , employed labourers who lived on the farm. After the Black Death any surviving labourers were able to better themselves by renting empty properties - the bedel rolls show that the income from the manor's rented property continued unchanged in the years after the plague – but there was a resulting shortage of hired labour on the farm.

The obvious conclusion is that that enormous hall had become far too big and far too expensive to maintain – and so the priory leased it – to William Horne.

Now, since the monks went on farming in Appledore, the monk wardens continued to visit the place, but their lodgings were no longer available and they were far too aristocratic to lodge in a peasant hovel. We can imagine their dismay and how they would arrange for new lodgings to be built for them as quickly as possible and how, if he would continue to let them use their accustomed chamber in the hall until their new house was built, say for one year, then they would allow William to hear mass with them in their chapel – an honour greater than we are able to understand today. Possibly this was even a condition imposed on the taking of the property but whatever the reason the licence was duly issued, its terms retained in perpetuity.

Although William was roosting in the hall, the bedel rolls show that the serjeant and bedel were continuing to run the farm just as they were before William erupted into their lives. The Hornes held a large acreage of Dover Priory land but I could find no definitive evidence of their renting a significant area of Christ Church land. Undoubtedly until the monks moved out in around 1379 they went on farming from their old demesne farm which, by now, was on its way to being renamed 'Horne's Place'. They retained their old farmyard which can be seen today - and still serves as a farmyard - just to the east of Horne's Place and separated from it by little more than a ditch. The bedel rolls mention a second chamber which was possibly sited in the great barn and still provided accommodation for the serjeant.

So there is no good reason for not supposing that Horne's Place was the site of the demesne farm until its removal to the village in 1379. Anyway, apart from this, there really is nowhere else that it could have been.

Our original quest was a castle and one that was burnt by the French. The French certainly came to Appledore in 1380 – although there is evidence that suggests it was actually a Spanish ship that sailed into Appledore - not that it made any difference for, French or Spanish, they were equally efficient in sacking and looting and they more or less destroyed Appledore. The bedel rolls show that the farm spent over £55 on rebuilding the barn and other buildings, market stalls were repaired, 15 new ones were made, and the priory itself contributed to the expense of restoration.

Appledore must still have been licking its wounds the following year when the Peasants' Revolt took place. William Horne does not appear to have endeared himself to the local populace for his dwelling was attacked twice, on 17 April and 19 April, and 'his houses (sic) were knocked down'.

On the 21 May in the following year, 1382, one of the largest earthquakes ever recorded in Kent shook the county. Amongst other damage it destroyed the campanile of Canterbury Cathedral, ruined the chancel of Hollingbourne church and disturbed the examination of Wycliffe for heresy in Blackfriars so that the trial was ever afterwards known as the Council of the Earthquake. It is thought that the epicentre was in east Kent but, unsurprisingly, there is little information about damage at Appledore. Presumably by now the inhabitants took destruction as 'par for the course'.

The French raid was by far the most dramatic of these events and so it would not be surprising if this was the story which Josephus Bloggs related to his wide-eyed grandchildren. After all, during the Peasants' Revolt it is more than likely that young Bloggs was knocking down Horne's houses with the rest of the lads so that to him this was just a bit of fun, a minor event compared with the drama of the foreign attack. But how did the castle come into it?

William Horne's 'houses' which were knocked down must have included the great hall of the original demesne farm and the documentary evidence suggests that this was a stone building as large as a church. There have been those who found it difficult to believe that there had ever been a very large stone hall here for in places where castles have been destroyed the stone is usually still to be seen in the walls of later buildings. This is not the case in Appledore.

Not surprisingly an explanation can be found in the bedel rolls. Between 1414 and 1415 the demesne farm was rented out to Nicholas Philip who is described as the superintendent of the walls and manorial *grange* – or barn. The walls specified were in fact the sea walls including the Great Wall of Appledore built to protect the marsh from flooding. Materials to maintain these walls were hard to come by, and during this year Nicholas bought 14 cartloads of stone from a local source which must surely have been Horne's

Place. Some might have been used for underpinning the barn walls but undoubtedly most would have disappeared into the sea defences.

Further evidence for the great stone hall at Horne's Place is given by Hasted towards the end of the eighteenth century. The owners of the house, he said, had dug up so many large stones in the garden that they were certain that there had once been a very big stone building there.

The existence of the stone hall seems well certified. Now the term 'castle' was used pretty loosely and did not necessarily mean the type of great defensive fort that is found, for example, on the Welsh borders. For the inhabitants of this swampy, forested region of Kent, the great hall of the demesne farm surrounded by its ancillary buildings would have had a certain mystique so that, after its demolition by the peasants (with probably a bit of help from the earthquake) it is not surprising if in time the descendants of Josephus Bloggs came to describe it as a great castle. And naturally it would not have been the action of a few neighbours but the devastating French raid that was memorable – so of course the destruction of the 'castle' was attributed to their wicked ways.

Simply: a great castle burnt down by the French.

And so we come to Sir John's second myth – the 'church now visible' that was 'not only repaired but, as some from ancient tradition affirm, wholly re-edified' from the castle ruins. Well, the existing chapel, as big as some churches, with its magnificent windows is enough to suggest that it fulfils the details of the second myth. However the windows are replacement windows in an older building and the question arises: was this chapel built from a ruined building, and was it indeed the chapel in which William was permitted to attend mass?

In fact the demesne farm possessed a chapel which was provided by Prior Eastry in 1291.The chapel remained at the farm until it was taken away in 1378 just before the farm moved to its new site in the village, so this would have been the chapel mentioned in the 1366 licence. It seems rather unlikely that William Horne would have had access to this chapel for his own private devotions and he may well have converted part of the hall to a small oratory. However the windows in the chapel today are mainly in the perpendicular style of the fifteenth century and almost certainly this marks the time when this building became a chapel.

South Wall of Chapel with gate above steps leading to undercroft door

Today if we look at its south wall we can see that the central part has been rebuilt with stone rubble contrasting with the fine ashlar used elsewhere. A plinth with a coping stone runs along the bottom of the east wall, returns along the south wall for a short distance and then stops at about the point where the wall has been rebuilt and directly below the east edge of the squint. It is a properly cut stop, not an accidental one, and shows that another wall was joined to the chapel at this point. This wall must have been part of some kind of extension but, because the doorway into the undercroft is only a short distance away, it cannot have been a large one. It might originally have housed the drain from a garde-robe but this seems unlikely because the door leading into it would have had a rather eye-catching position near the middle of the chamber wall and such doors were usually tucked away in an inconspicuous corner.

There is another alternative and perhaps a more likely one, namely that it was a chimney.

Roughly halfway up this south wall there is a small square glassed-in opening which is called 'the squint'. Squints were holes built into church walls to allow people, lepers for example, to see the elevation of the Host at mass. Since your leper would have to be some ten feet tall to look through this squint it seems a rather odd place for it although it is possible that the afore-mentioned extension provided a viewing platform. A more important objection to the theory that this was a squint is the fact that this was a pre-reformation private chapel and the celebration of mass in it was severely restricted. A licence similar to the 1366 licence would have been needed and had such a licence been issued it is likely that a record of it would have survived. Certainly a number of such licences connected with other private oratories are still in existence today. Of course this is uncertain – but one thing is sure: when those windows turned the chamber into a private oratory the owner would have been well aware that mass would not be a routine event in it, that there would rarely if ever be an elevation of the Host to be witnessed through a squint and the provision of such a facility was pointless.

In fact, the squint actually looks more like part of the opening from a fireplace into a chimney. Such a chimney would have been exactly the right size and in the right place to form that small extension. If such a hearth and chimney existed they would indicate that the room had been designed for the accommodation of a VIP, namely the prior. Certainly he visited the manor from time to time, considerable sums were spent on his entertainment and the bedel rolls refer more than once to the prior's chamber.

In Hollingbourne, another Christ Church manor, the bedel roll for 1369 -1370 describes how a metal worker was employed to make a new iron flue for the chimney of the prior's chamber. When the new stone manor house was built in Great Chart in 1312-1313 a chimney was built into the hall there. Although even the better-heeled relations of the Bloggs family had to wait until the sixteenth century for the comfort of a chimney some 200 years earlier they were commonplace for the jet-setting monastic elite.

They were, nevertheless, the ultimate luxury and when those peasants came along you can imagine how their grievances would have been exacerbated at the sight of this status symbol. It would have been a prime target for their hostile action. While the chimney is speculative, the existence and the destruction of the south wall and that small extension cannot be doubted and clearly this came about before the rebuilding of the wall. So, judging by those windows, the chapel came into being after the damage and the repairs had been done.

There does not seem at present to be any record of how, why or when the glassed-in squint was made. Was it left as an ornament or was it filled in with ragstone when the south wall was repaired? If so, maybe at some time unspecified the stones gave way, the cut stone at the side of the hole was revealed (it appears to have thirteenth century type stone-dressing) and the hole was opened up as a feature of the building. Just 'maybe'!

There is one other mystery – the site of the original door into the chamber. Today one enters through what can only be described as a crudely cut hole in the west wall. In the north wall there is a properly constructed but now blocked doorway which connected with the rebuilt house and in the south wall, at the bottom of some steps, there is a first-build doorway into the undercroft. The chapel floor cuts across the top of the undercroft windows, which are properly set into the ashlar showing that they are not insertions, and this suggests that the chapel floor was originally higher than it is today. If it were, then it increases the possibility that the 'squint' was part of a fireplace and led into a chimney. However, it raises questions about that doorway leading into the house from this floor level – were the floor and this doorway part of the rebuilding and formation of the chapel? Was there a doorway here anyway before the reconstruction? Was it in the south wall and destroyed by the attacks in the Peasants' Revolt? Is it possible that the entrance was via a stairway from the undercroft? (Probably not because it contains a well). And when will the solutions to these problems be revealed – a challenge to future architectural historians!

Maybe the earthquake ended Horne's love affair with great stone houses. By 1414 the stone hall had gone and presumably the new timber framed house that replaced it had been planned or built. It was probably at the same time that the chamber was rebuilt and fitted out with the latest and most ostentatious windows available to produce a chapel of such grandeur that the locals regarded it as a church – the 'church now visible' that was 'not only repaired but, as some from ancient tradition affirm, wholly re-edified' from the castle ruins'.

By studying the topography, the built environment and the contemporary documents of Appledore we have found that there is a good foundation for the myth if we accept the necessity of looking at the past in the terms of the past and not the present. That the original demesne farmhouse, the great stone *aule*, became Horne's Place and that Prior Eastry moved the demesne or manor farm to a new site near Appledore church, where it remains today as the Court Lodge is to all intents and purposes an incontrovertible theory. An inspection of the structure of the chapel at Horne's Place today adds convincing evidence to support the hypothesis that Horne's Place is the site of the Appledore Myth.

* * * * *

The Mystery of the Wandering Chapel

The chapel that stood at Horne's Place had been built by Henry Eastry, the prior, in 1291 at a cost of £3 5s 8½d. This was no great sum of money and suggests that the chapel was a small timber built structure, a fact that agrees with the information that a chapel was 'dragged' to a new site in 1378. It must have been a sturdy little building but even so the mind boggles at the thought of moving it from A to B with fourteenth century technology. It can't have gone far! The mystery is: where exactly did it come to rest and what eventually happened to it?

It would have been given a position of honour close to the hall when it was first built. The farm *curia* or courtyard lay to the east of the hall and today accommodates the modern barns belonging to Gusbourne Farm. The farm probably took its name from the up-and-coming Gosbonie family. There was a 'Richard Gosbonie near Horne's Mill' in 1472 and – medieval leases being what they were – it is likely that his family had taken over the farm when the priory forsook it. Although today the farmhouse, a Victorian structure, stands on rising ground to the east, the previous farmhouse was still standing on the south-east edge of the farm yard until the middle of the twentieth century and might possibly have contained remnants of that 1367 *coquinna*. When they set about dragging the chapel to a new site they would not have pulled it eastwards into the old farmyard nor is it likely that they would have tugged it uphill on to the mill bank or on to the rising ground to the north. In fact, looking at the surrounding countryside, it seems most likely that it was hauled along the surviving road in a westerly direction to a point where two ancient tracks cross. Today, in the middle of the crossroads here, there is quite a large fenced in area where a timber-framed cottage stands and it is tempting to think that this was where the chapel came to rest.

Wherever it was, it was cherished. It was underpinned with stone and lime, the walls plastered and lime-washed and although it had previously been thatched it was now re-roofed with 1000 tiles. It was obviously a small building and it was enclosed and protected by a paling fence. A new cope chest had been made for it and this suggests that the monk wardens from Canterbury continued to celebrate mass in it after its translation.

From surviving wills we learn that in 1470 James Marchall bequeathed four pence to the Chapel of St James on the Heath and on 25 June 1509 John Combe left a sum of 3s 4d to the chapel of St Jacob (an alternative form of James). Another will, that of Robert Heuxsted in 1524, gives 6s 8d for the repair of 'the highway between the Chapel and the Crosse in Apuldre strete' showing that the chapel stood beside the highway leading into Appledore street but some distance away – 6s 8d should have mended quite a stretch of road. It seems therefore that the demesne farm chapel had become the chapel of St James on the Heath. Perhaps a hermit took up residence in it at one time for in her will of 1495 Joane Kelett left a sum of four pence to the 'hermit of the Heath'.

There is nothing to suggest that the cross roads was not a possible location for the chapel but equally, apart from the lie of the land, there is nothing to confirm this. Clearly, wherever the chapel was, it was well cared for up to the time of the Dissolution of the Monasteries but the suppression of Christ Church Priory meant that the monk wardens no longer came to Appledore and celebrated mass in it. The little chapel now came into the possession of the Dean and Chapter of Canterbury Cathedral, another religious body, who probably felt obliged to treat it with some respect, yet were loath to spend money on a building for which they had no use.

Some monastic property was bought and used by laymen for up-market housing, so was the little chapel converted to a dwelling or was it moved it again, releasing the ground for a more profitable building? Looking again at the fenced-in ground at the cross roads with roads running all round it, the house known as Roundabout Friday (because at one time the dilatory builder employed for repairs always said that he could resume work 'round about Friday') has been dated to about 1600. Careful examination of the property reveals no sign of an earlier building incorporated in the fabric and it appears to have been new-built a short time after the Dissolution. Could it have been put up after the chapel had been moved away from the site and if this was the case, where did the chapel go now?

The Dean and Chapter continued the priory's habit of renting out land and properties and some of the leases are still in existence. However, leases were no longer the open-ended arrangements of earlier days but had become much more formal with fixed terms, lists of the properties involved and various conditions stipulated. One dated 30 September 1581 lists shops, including two ruinous ones, soil and ground in Appledore market place, an acre of woodland and the rights to the annual fair all of which was rented out to Henry Elmeston on a 21 year lease at a rent of three pounds per annum. He was obliged to rebuild or repair the shops within a year and maintain buildings and fences, and was not permitted to fell 'timber' trees.

The next surviving lease in this series is dated 26 January 1620/1 (whether the new year should start on 25 March in the traditional way, or on 1 January was under consideration) and again was a 21 year lease issued to John Morly, There were two differences from the previous one: the rent had fallen to 25 shillings per annum, but – more interestingly – he was now given the use of the 'Crosse House or house in the market place' together with firm instructions to keep the Crosse House in repair. A later lease gives the lessee permission to use it to lay in the boards and poles used for the fair and the market, and 'to make the house habitable if he desires'.

This Crosse House which materialised in the market place between 1581 and 1620 seems to have been a strange little place. It was obviously the property of the Dean and Chapter who lavished a considerable amount of attention on its upkeep. A survey of Court Lodge and its outbuildings was carried out in 1637 when the great barn was found to be in a sad state of repair but the 'market house and Chappell' were both 'very well and lately repaired and built'. A later document shows that the Crosse House had two separate compartments and maybe the term 'built' in the expression 'lately repaired and built' indicates that the building had been recently extended. Sundry documents show that the terms 'Market House' and 'Crosse House' were used indiscriminately for the same building, but this reference to a chapel in relation to the Crosse House is interesting. When the Court Lodge was built it was no longer designed to be a monastic residence and no chapel was included on the site.

It is assumed that it was called the Crosse House because it was situated near the village cross, but is it possible that the name arose because the building had been moved to the village from the cross roads? Or was a cross set on the roof to show its sacred origin?

The Crosse House finally disappeared in 1830. In her notes for a lecture to be given in the 1930s a certain Miss Rogers writes about the Crosse House: 'On the green patch opposite Miss Mollett's house there used to be a little wooden lodge called the Cross House or chapel which was originally a Prayer house'. Elsewhere she says that it came down from medieval times and that it had been used to hold the ropes and stakes for the annual fair. One end was the shop of a local shoemaker.

On the whole the medieval church was not keen on chapels and they did not proliferate across the countryside in the way that non-conformist chapels did after the Act of Toleration. Chantry chapels, usually in churches, where a priest was employed to sing; private oratories where the very sick might obtain a licence to hear mass; or a Chapel of Ease for those who lived in a hamlet judged to be beyond walking distance of a church and for which a licence was needed, these were permitted but the restrictions were stringent. This restraint means that it was unlikely that there were a lot of chapels littered around the countryside, and therefore it seems quite possible that Miss Rogers's 'little wooden lodge called the Crosse House or chapel which was originally a Prayer house' was the chapel originally built by Prior Eastry for his monks at the demesne farm.

Whether it ever stood on the site of Roundabout Friday is a matter of speculation. Perhaps one day archaeologists will be able to solve the problem.

* * * * *

The Mystery of the 'Mound'

Just south of Horne's Place the ground rises to a low ridge overlooking Romney Marsh. This ridge is known as the Mill Bank and to reach it you follow a track that leads due south past the gateway into the Horne's Place chapel and on beside a stretch of water. It then swings round towards the east, continues up through a steep little hollow-way and comes out on to an area of high ground. The 'mound' rises up a few yards away and from it a footpath runs down into Appledore village.

The Mound from the South with the Footpath to the Village

This was certainly the site of the windmill which, probably because of its proximity to Horne's Place, was called Horne's Mill in a bedel roll of 1472. Earlier it must have been the mill attached to the demesne farm and the bedel rolls show that it needed constant repair. Prior Eastry's Memorandum Book records the building of the mill in 1305 at a cost of £16 2s 5d. It was probably not finished much before 1307 when canvas was purchased for the sails and a rope bought 'to hold the mill'. There is, however, a mill mentioned in the first bedel roll of 1265 and clearly this one predates Eastry's mill. Therefore there were probably two mills on this site although there is nothing to suggest that the older mill survived the construction of the new one. When all artefacts were scarce and expensive it seems likely that the old mill was taken down and anything of value was salvaged from it although it may have continued in use until the new mill was completed.

This new mill had an earth fast post and was lightly constructed with *wat wogh* (wattle walls) which were mended with *schotbord* or wooden battens fixed in place with nails. The working parts which are listed for repairs include a *spyndel* (spindle) a *mattok,* a bill for which iron was needed, *trand-stavas* (cross beams) a *trendella* (trundle wheel), cogs and cogwheels and a lantern wheel with cogs and a *drofbeam*.

In 1383 the mill needed a lot of structural repairs. Men were given food and drink (normal wages for casual labour) for lifting and carrying mill posts and other timber to it. One man was paid 4s 2d for digging round the post of the mill which had obviously been quite badly damaged but who knows whether it was by the French raid, the peasants or the earthquake? In the following year the internal machinery of the mill was extensively renovated and renewed and the miller was taken to Folkestone to choose a new mill-stone which was eventually brought up to Appledore by boat. The total cost of the stone was £2 14s. A second mill-stone was brought down from Canterbury at a cost of only 12d. Further work on the site consisted of the building of a large new thatched pig-sty near the mill.

By the beginning of the fifteenth century the mill was leased out to a tenant and a new mill was built in 1480 by John Stylle on the high ground now called Mill Hill which lies to the west of Court Lodge. Today a small circle of raised ground shows the site of this mill. However the old mill near Horne's

Place was still being repaired in 1484 when it was called the *antique molendium.*

Today the mound is the subject of much curiosity. It is huge and much too large for the type of mound on which mills were often built. In any case, since these very early windmills had earth fast posts they would need to be set on the ground and not on built-up piles of earth.

Exactly when the mill was first leased out is uncertain but by 1384 the miller was a tenant paying an annual rent of £3 for the mill and this probably included the rent of a house for he would certainly have needed to live close to the mill. As early as 1318 a bedel roll mentions 'mending' a shop but without any details to show what sort of building this was. Then there was that pig-sty where pigs thrived on waste from the grinding process and would have been a nice little earner – although maybe not for the miller. Indeed there must have been some kind of settlement up here near the mill, and this has left no trace today. Unless, of course, the remains of it are buried under the mound.

The mill is shown on the map of Kent produced by Phil. Symonson (gent) of Rochester in 1596. The following year he became mayor of Rochester - had he travelled around Kent and actually seen that the mill was still in existence at this time? It is not shown on Speed's map of 1610. However around this period the mill certainly became redundant and the settlement, such as it was, was abandoned. Anything serviceable would have been removed for use elsewhere but how much material could be recycled from the old mill itself is questionable.

As the site became more derelict we can imagine how the remains of the pigsty and the 'shop', the rotting canvas from the sailyards and the *schotbord* from the mill would have littered the site and how the brambles and nettles that spring up so quickly on waste ground would have taken over. Two courses of action were possible – leaving the site for nature to convert into an untidy patch of woodland, or clearing away the rubbish and – maybe - burning it. It would have been a big bonfire probably built over the remains of the mill itself or even over two mills if odd bits of the earlier one remained. Could the remains of such a pile of rubbish or bonfire be the foundation of the mound?

Perhaps one day excavation will find the answer.

* * * * *

More Mysteries

The castle and church, the chapel and the windmills all have their own veil of mystery – and there are others. Appledore might be described as Kent's most mysterious village.

Next is the mystery of the 'brotherhood of Apuldre' (Appledore). They appear as witnesses of the Heronden Charter of 968, and the term 'brethren' suggests that they inhabited some kind of conventual establishment. However in 697 a list was made of the monasteries existing in Kent at this time and Appledore is not among those mentioned. If it somehow escaped recognition at this stage it is unlikely that it would have escaped the attention of the Danish invaders of 893. Monasteries at Minster, Hoo and Sheppey, for example, were destroyed by the Danes, and since their activities on the Kent Coast continued on and off until after the Norman Conquest, it is unlikely that anyone would have been foolhardy enough to set up a new monastery for them to knock down.

Appledore manor had certainly come into the possession of Christ Church by the end of Canute's reign in 1035 – or possibly even by 1006 - and their records give no evidence of a monastery here. It has been suggested that the brethren were the monks and their servants who were engaged in managing the Appledore manor farm.

While Horne's Place was certainly the Christ Church manor farm in the thirteenth century and may well have been so since the eleventh century, the possibility that this was not the original Appledore demesne farm site should not be discounted. A church is mentioned in the *Domesday Monachorum* and there is no reason to suppose that the existing church does not stand on the site of this pre-conquest church. It was the possession of Dover Priory and it has been suggested that the little chapel on the north-east side of the church could have Saxon origins. Since a demesne farm was usually close to the church it may be that the farm inhabited by the brethren in 968 was close to the church. However, the area round the church and the village street has been almost entirely rebuilt over the centuries and any trace of such a farm is not going to be easy to find.

Alternatively, the monks who farmed at what became Horne's Place may have been continuing a tradition that dated back to the tenth century. Farmland to the north of Horne's Place belongs to Gusborne Farm and in the woodland bordering this land a rather overgrown pond has been identified as a man-made construction and tentatively described as a monastic fish pond.

Then, not long ago in one of these fields a large buried hoard of pre-conquest coins was discovered. They came from a very wide area and were therefore thought to have been in the possession of a travelling merchant who buried them for safe-keeping while on his travels. Was he a guest of the monks who ran the manor farm? For if so it adds credence – however slight – to the belief that Horne's Place is a residence still in use on a site where men have lived for over a thousand years.

And finally – where was the port at Appledore where visitors disembarked, where the miller's mill-stone was landed and other goods brought in? For a number of years the Romney Marsh Research Trust ran a Small Ports Project which looked for the sites and possible remains of the harbours associated with this area. There was certainly a port in Appledore, and extensive research suggests that it was near the foot of the bank on which Stylle built his windmill. Sadly the cutting of the Royal Military Canal has destroyed any evidence of it and at present it appears difficult to see how this question can be answered.

* * * * *

WESTWELL

The Legend of Westwell Monastery

The Westwell Legend is a very simple one; it merely states that Court Lodge was once a monastery. Today, as you look at the front of the house you see a fine Victorian villa that seems inclined to turn its nose up at any suggestion of a monastic connection. However, if you walk up the path beside the house to the church, and look over the churchyard wall at the back wall of the house you see a very different building. This, until recently, boasted a lancet window which was set in fabric identical to that of the church walls so that it seems obvious that the church and the back portion of the house were built at the same time. But was it a monastery? That word suggests a complex of several buildings providing dormitories, kitchens, refectories, accommodation for visitors and for the old and infirm, not to mention fishponds and gardens. The church and house built close together here at Westwell would scarcely seem to deserve the title of Monastery. On the other hand, builders didn't go to the expense of fine windows and stone walls for a mason's lodge or a priest's house. This house was a high status dwelling and built for a specific purpose – what?

Now, if it did have some kind of monastic connection this would have ended in the reign of Henry VIII so we would expect to find references to it prior to the dissolution. Westwell, like Appledore, was a manor owned by Christ Church Priory and so there are bedel rolls from which we can deduce some of the manor history. It seems that these bedel rolls were stored at the bottom of the pile and were more available to insects and dirt and such like so that their condition makes many of them unreadable. Fortunately not all!

Westwell Church from the Court Lodge Gateway

One of the earlier ones, dating to 1291-1292, is particularly valuable for amongst a welter of building expenses it uses the term *nova berthona* which means new farm, the farm in this context meaning the demesne farm. It goes on to tell us how the manorial barn was taken down and moved to this new site. Before this could be done the ground had to be levelled to accommodate it and more ground was levelled for an enormous new ox-house. In addition a new mill, a water-mill in this case, was built. Prior Eastry arranged that Christ Church Priory should bear most of the expense of these buildings and in 1292 it paid out a sum of over £49 for the work done on the barn and ox-house and, with the cost of the new mill and sundry small buildings, the total bill was over £67.

These buildings were not thatched but were from the beginning tiled with tiles actually made in Westwell. The tileworks continued to produce tiles and to sell them to other manors in the locality until around 1310.

It was usual for a barn to be put up before a start was made on the construction of an important house but in this case there is no record of the building of a new house. Since a farmhouse was an essential feature of the farm it is reasonable to suppose that a house already existed on the site and this must have been that part of the Court Lodge which was built at the same time as the church. So we can be pretty sure that the Court Lodge was taken over as a farmhouse in around 1292, but clearly the house existed before the farm moved to this site, so it does not explain the previous use of the house or answer the question about its monastic claims.

Today Westwell, despite its charm, seems a strange little village neither dawdling down a village street nor clustering around a village green. There are just a few small roads meandering around it. The Court Lodge stands beside the church and across the road a great brick-built barn still lords it over a courtyard where once the manorial barn and ox-house stood in the farm *curia*. This modern barn has now

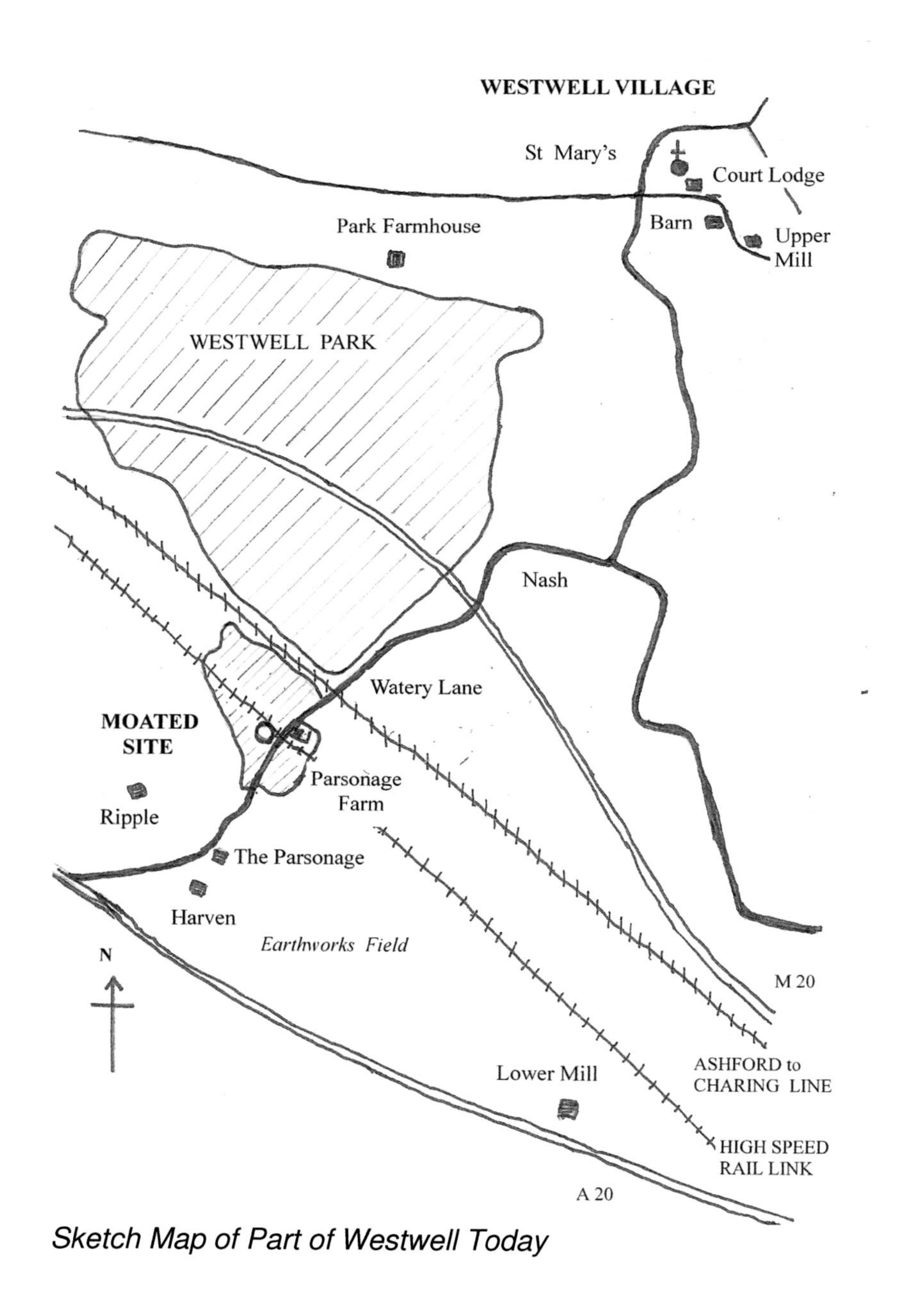

Sketch Map of Part of Westwell Today

been converted to dwellings although it was still in agricultural use until the middle of the twentieth century. A short walk down the road brings you to the mill which Prior Eastry commissioned. Despite the rebuilding of the mill house it remains an over-shot mill and until shortly before the end of the twentieth century the mill wheel drove a generator which supplied electricity to the house.

As far as the early history of Westwell is concerned there is the Domesday Book which reveals the presence of a mill and the Domesday Monachorum which shows that there was a pre-Conquest church here. Further information on these buildings is provided by an archaeological exploration made prior to the construction of the high-speed rail link. Some mile and a half south of the existing village there is a house called Parsonage Farm which was once known as the Old Rectory. Close to this but separated from it by a road and a stream, the Museum of London archaeologists uncovered the remains of a moated house. They were restricted to a very shallow excavation which did not disturb the subsoil because the high speed rail link was to be built directly above it. At the lowest level which they were permitted to reach they found traces of possible late iron-age or Roman occupation and what appeared to be a later mill leat. This could well be associated with the mill mentioned in the Domesday Book. Above this they found the remains of a timber hall with a stone solar at the east end and ancillary buildings which would have included an external kitchen. At this time the stream to the east of these buildings had not been extended to form the moat. After about 1250 the old hall was replaced by a larger aisled one with an improved solar and bigger service buildings and the moat was completed. This was a rather fine dwelling and from their findings they were able to show that the house had been occupied by apparently well-heeled owners until nearly the end of the fourteenth century. At this point it was demolished. One rather surprising fact was that all the materials from the dismantled house had been taken away from the site and almost as surprising was the huge number of broken tiles that still littered the ground.

Is there a possibility that this was the site of the Westwell Monastery, its situation having been mistaken in rather the same way that the Appledore Myth has long been associated with Appledore parish church instead of Horne's Place? Once again those useful bedel rolls provide an answer.

By 1400 the priory was leasing out its land in Westwell although the bedel still kept the accounts because the priory continued to finance certain capital works on the farm. In Westwell the demesne (or manor) farm and the rectory (or glebe) farm were treated as two separate holdings, sometimes rented by a single tenant, sometimes by two. The bedel roll for 1402-1403 records the removal of 34 cartloads of old timber carried from Westwell *Rectoria* (Rectory) to the manor, and 11,000 flat tiles (taken) from the said Rectory to the manor. At this time the term 'manor' meant the Court Lodge farm and these entries accord so well with the archaeological findings, namely that the materials were removed from the site of the moated house after its destruction in around 1400, that they establish the fact that the moated house was Westwell Rectory and must have been so for a long time. It had no monastic pretensions.

There is no record of stones from the solar being carried to the manor and they are presumably the ones still in business incorporated in a barn and supporting a bank beside Parsonage Farm on the far side of the road.

In this bedel roll there is one further entry which states that 12,000 tiles (were) taken from the old building in the outer courtyard. The archaeological remit only allowed the exploration of the area inside the moat – the inner court - where just domestic buildings were found. This outer courtyard must have been the farmyard, for the moated house was situated in the middle of the glebe farm, and the old building, which had been tiled, was probably the barn which we would know as the tithe barn. These tiles were deposited in the Rectory until, in 1403 – 1404, 11,000 of them were taken to Great Chart. It must have been many of the remaining 1000 tiles – broken and useless - which the archaeologists found littering the site.

Obviously the question arises: why on earth did the priory decide to demolish the rectory and the great tithe barn?

The parish rector was a man of some importance who received the great tithe and the income from the glebe farm, and was responsible for the upkeep of the chancel in the parish church. For many years Christ Church Priory had held the advowson of the Westwell benefice which meant that they could appoint whoever they chose, either a priest or a layman, to be rector. Then, in 1397, they themselves appropriated the church meaning that the priory assumed the role of rector and grabbed the great tithe. Clearly the priory, being an institution and not a man, did not need a house in Westwell, and if the priory coffers were to be benefit from the tithe there was no need for a tithe barn. Since there is evidence to show that there had not been a rector living in the rectory since 1328 maybe the house and buildings were falling into disrepair anyway.

Since a rector was not necessarily in holy orders villages were often served by a *vicarius* (substitute) priest or vicar who was provided with a vicarage and the small tithe, probably not much more than a pittance. In Westwell the first vicar was introduced in 1293 and, as vicar, did not have to bear the expense of repairing the chancel. However, after the priory had assumed the role of rector in 1411, it did just that. Actually it palmed the work off on to its tenant farmer, James Fox, who claimed £1 10s 9d for the lime, sand and timber that he had had to buy - while it was his workmen who had to tackle the job.

Now undoubtedly the rectory had originally housed the parish priests who, prior to the reformation, would have been obliged to recite the appointed offices in the church throughout the day. This means that the early church must have stood near to the rectory for the priests could not have run back and forth to a church situated a mile and a half away where the existing church stands. Since the pre-conquest church would certainly have been situated near the heart of the community we must assume that Westwell with its manor and lesser dwellings was originally a considerable distance south of the village we see today. The archaeological findings suggest that there was once a mill on the site and this was replaced by the Lower Mill which is a short distance away to the east. However this was a secular community and there is no sign of a monastery hereabouts.

So, returning to Court Lodge and the church there – why was this second church needed – and so far away from the first one?

John Newman, writing in the esteemed Pevsner Guide, considers that this church was built all at once in the thirteenth century and that the tower arch could not be earlier than 1250. Simon Jenkins in 'England's Thousand Best Churches' describes the location of the church in the following terms: 'A pilgrim's church nestles under the Downs'.

The word 'pilgrim' is suggestive, for following the murder of Thomas a Becket in 1170 his shrine in Canterbury became a major attraction for pilgrims. Chaucer's *Canterbury Tales* tells stories of pilgrims coming down the London to Dover road, but undoubtedly there were visitors from the west who came along the ancient track which became known as the Pilgrim's Way in the nineteenth century. It runs along the lower slopes of the North Downs, a lonely little lane that avoids contact with humanity over long stretches of countryside. One can imagine travellers getting more and more hungry, thirsty

Interior of Westwell Church

and weary as they journeyed on, and their feelings of relief when they saw ahead of them the welcoming tower of Charing church. Beside it stood the great palace belonging to the Archbishop where he came with his cavalcade of servants and where the great and the good were entertained. It was a busy place with its farm and fine banqueting halls and lodgings and, sadly, a place where pilgrims would be about as welcome as back-packers would be in Buckingham Palace today. But, unlike our Queen, monastic establishments were obliged to provide lodgings for travellers. So did the Archbishop decide that the best way of keeping hoards of pilgrims out of his hair was to provide them with a hostel a mile or so further down the road; a nice church and lodging house kept by the monks where they could be provided with refreshment for body, mind and soul?

It certainly looks as if this could have been the case. The church built soon after the death of Thomas a Becket is incredibly beautiful although it is so badly built in parts that it still needs constant upkeep; it is a mixture of wonderful design but a lot of actual construction seems to have been done in a hurry using unskilled labour. The house was built at the same time and could therefore be a sort of Maison Dieu run by monks to provide the food and lodging needed by the pilgrims and passing travellers. In these circumstances it is possible to understand how the Bloggs family came to associate the place with a monastery.

And, of course, when Prior Eastry was bustling around in his efforts to improve his farms and make them more profitable, it is not surprising that he looked at this fine, newly built house and decided that a few alterations would turn it into a comfortable farmhouse where a few pilgrims could be given a nights B&B if necessary.

Again this is theory built on putting together all the information available and one which fits all the facts known at present. Therefore, until new evidence appears we can believe that it is not far from the truth.

* * * * *

Another Mystery

The actual site of old Westwell, the pre-Conquest church and the original demesne farm is an ongoing mystery and a lot of new work needs to be done to find them. Railways and motorways have proliferated and buried so much archaeology that a lot of information has been lost forever.

An important thing to remember about the Kent Countryside is the fact that a great deal of it was owned by various ecclesiastical bodies including Christ Church Priory, St Augustine's Abbey, Dover Priory, Battle Abbey and also by the Archbishop at Canterbury Cathedral, and the Bishop of Rochester. The main purpose of this land was to feed the communities attached to these bodies and maintain them in some luxury (which seems to have borne little relationship to the monastic vows of poverty, chastity and obedience.)

The countryside was divided up into manor farms which produced the food, but where the farm was far away from the parent body it was found more profitable to rent it out (with the proviso that it should provide hospitality for its respective prior or bishop if said dignitary was visiting the locality). This was certainly the case with *Welles* (Westwell) for it was leased out to a certain Peter de Bending.

This unfortunate and foolish gentleman ran into cash-flow problems which were made infinitely worse when he looked for help from Jewish moneylenders. To pay his debts to them he first gave up the Westwell manor for the smaller, cheaper Little Chart holding and them had to relinquish that as well.

While he was still holding Westwell manor he presumably lived in the manor house and in view of his financial position probably paid less attention to repairs than he should have done. It may well be that the house had become pretty dilapidated by the time Prior Eastry took control of the farm and this contributed to the removal of the farm to its new site. There is nothing to indicate what happened to this old house, but it does not exist today and so must have been taken down.

At first the excavation of the moated house seemed to suggest that the missing manor house had been located. However, there is no doubt that this house, situated in the middle of the Glebe farm, was the rectory and it seems unlikely that it had led a double life as the manor house as well.

We know that the *Rectoria,* set on its moated island, had an outer courtyard and that a large tiled building, which we have identified as the tithe barn, had stood there. The archaeologists found two bridges across the moat, one leading to the north and on to land that rose up gently towards the Park, the other to the east where it led on to the road, (Station Road aka Watery Lane). Towards the east and on the far side of the road the ground rises steeply so the outer courtyard probably lay to the north and abutted on to the Park.

The Saxon church would not have been far from the priest's house or Rectory, and is thought to have belonged to a secondary group of mother churches or minsters so that it would have been quite an important place and would have been at the heart of the community at the time when it was built.

Returning to the bedel rolls we find a reference to the repair of the *Ecclesia* or parish church in 1411 but there are also several references to a *Capella* or chapel. It was a building of some importance for in 1299 the serjeant, Adam atte Gater, charged for four days work plastering and tiling the chapel and for making two new doors for it. Research has not revealed the existence of any free chapel, chantry chapel or chapel belonging to a manor in Westwell and the fact that it needed two doors is significant. While a private oratory would normally need only one door a church always had a north and south door – so was this chapel the still surviving Saxon church, demoted to the status of a chapel after the building of the new Pilgrim's church?

And where was it situated? Prior Eastry in 1287 mentions a new gate into the Park by the chapel, and in 1481 Jacob Ryman, who was renting the Rectory Farm claims for the expense of making a gate into the Park near the street (presumably Watery Lane) and for making a door for the chapel there. These records seem to establish the situation of the chapel on rectory land, near to the road and a gateway into the park which must have been close to the outer court of the rectory.

Almost opposite to the place where the bridge from the moated house met the road a hollow way runs up the side of the hill and emerges beside the artificially levelled platform on which the sixteenth century Parsonage Farm house stands today. The farmhouse is awkwardly set on the very edge of the platform leaving the centre region bare and it is not conceivable that so much effort could have been expended on providing a site for this relatively unimportant dwelling. Could this have been the site of the Saxon church? It is certainly rather a wild guess and yet, in the Meon Valley near Winchester where church building went on apace before the Conquest and stone-built churches still remain, there are many cases that seem to illustrate a tradition for setting the church on a level site on the hillside above the dwellings that clustered beside a stream in the valley below. Not unlike the arrangement here in Westwell where it would originally have looked down on the mill with the mill-leat found by the archaeologists.

Whether there is any truth in this supposition or not, there is no doubt that the Saxon church was situated in this area, and that the old community and the old manor house would have been somewhere around here.

Harven

A little to the south of the old rectory site is Harven, a fine sixteenth century house. Stone walls surrounding a yard contain moulded stones which could have come from an earlier dwelling and the house is built on a plinth of similar stones. The interior is decorated with early wall paintings and the arms of Queen Elizabeth I are painted over the hearth in an upstairs chamber. Following an enquiry into the possible reason for the painting of the queen's arms, David Starkey kindly replied that it did not necessarily mean that the queen actually visited the house. The coat of arms might have been commissioned to celebrate Elizabeth's Progress round Kent in 1573 when she stayed nearby at Hothfield or, alternatively, it could have been done to indicate support for her and her religious policies. It does, however, suggest that this was an important house, the home of an influential villager. There were in Westwell several minor manors of which this was not one. Could its importance have devolved from the fact that it was the original demesne farm house? Much research would be needed to establish whether this was the case, it is nevertheless a distinct possibility and a point of interest.

Slightly to the north is another house now called the Parsonage and here the owners have found the remains of building work under one part of the garden and signs in another part that animals were kept here for a long period of time. To the east of Harven is a field in which humps and bumps and dry hollow ways appear similar to those left behind by a deserted medieval village. This field, situated between Harven and the Lower mill is also a little south of the fields where brickworks were established at a later date. Since this is the region where brick earth occurs it is not unreasonable to suppose that the thirteenth century tile works were in this area and that the men engaged in making the tiles lived nearby.

Such villages were often forsaken after the Black Death – could that have been the case here? The bedel rolls with the farm accounts would be extremely interesting in that they would show if the farm income had decreased substantially after the Black Death. In Appledore, while there are no accounts surviving for the two years following the Black Death, the succeeding ones show that the bedel continued to collect exactly the same rents as he had done before the plague. Clearly the death toll had not emptied the countryside as it had done in some parts of the country. For Westwell from the Black Death until 1364 there are only two rolls in very poor condition surviving and from these little information can be obtained. Maybe this in itself suggests that here the disease exacted a much heavier toll and led to the abandonment of the old village and its migration to its present site.

Field with Earthworks

Who knows? Perhaps one day archaeologists may be able to investigate some of these places and discover the site of Welles – the original Westwell.

* * * * *

The Legend of the Demon Archer

Westwell boasts another, more romantic legend, that of the Demon Archer of Westwell, a gentleman allegedly possessed of satanic powers.

The supernatural is, of course, the very stuff of legend. That it was accepted on a very prosaic level was revealed to me by the oddest thing that my grand-mother ever told me. I was, I expect, being at my most aggravating, airing my nine-year-old opinions of the world and its ways. "I ought not," my grandmother said, "to talk about things that I did not understand." In her younger days, she told me, she had actually known of a woman who could turn herself into a rat and who, in this form, would run through the attics of the row of cottages where she lived. This allowed her, the rat-woman, to get into the cottages and poke around in them whenever she wished. Grandma was born in 1854 (or thereabouts), had deep religious convictions and was a very down-to-earth person with little imagination and – in the ordinary way - a great deal of common sense. I didn't dare to ask her who had told her this story for though she seemed to think that it was a very educational one, I was forbidden to talk about it.

The legend of the Archer tells of a rascally duke who, in pursuance of his own nefarious ends, set a penny piece on the head of a small boy and, while taunting his father, ordered him to take his long bow and shoot the penny. The father, aided by those supernatural powers, sent the penny flying, took a second arrow and aimed it at the ducal heart. It is not clear whether the duke escaped or not, but the father went down in history as the Demon Archer of Westwell and his ghost is said to give warning of approaching death.

Doubtless the Bloggs family, like my grandmother, had acquaintances with unusual habits and thought nothing of the possession of satanic powers. The supernatural element can be ignored, but how did the legend begin? Did J. Bloggs senior ever witness an incident that could have initiated it? With most of the countryside under monastic control, wicked Dukes would seem to be in short supply. Had he heard the tale of William Tell? Discounting the satanic powers, the legend bears a striking resemblance to this famous account. Pilgrims travelled long distances and Chaucer bears witness to a story-telling culture. Or did the statute requiring the country's menfolk to practice with their long bows at the butts after church on Sundays and holidays inspire a competitive sport that spawned such stories?

The Willliam Tell yarn is believed to be apocryphal and if this was the source of the legend then it becomes understandable that with the passing of time the young Bloggses would have believed that Great-granddad's story referred to the place that they knew. This is not a myth that can be interpreted by chasing round the countryside, but it still is interesting if it leads us to think about village folk and the recreations that they enjoyed, whether listening to and telling yarns or competing in what must have become the football of the day.

They weren't all that different from us!

* * * * *

TENTERDEN AND SMALLHYTHE

The Tenterden Legend

The Tenterden Legend is a very simple one. It merely says that William Caxton, who introduced printing into England, was born in Tenterden.

Now archaeology, topography and the built environment are not much help when it comes to determining who was born where, and to investigate legends which are solely concerned with the whereabouts of a human being is not easy – unless that human was of a very exalted rank - for documentary sources are the only really useful ones. While Caxton certainly became an historic eminence he didn't actually start that way so, while we know quite a lot about his later life, there is little to show where it started.

The most important evidence is what he has to say himself: *'I was born and lerned myn englissh in Kente in the weeld where I doubte not is spoken as brode and rude englishh as is in ony place of englond.'* This does give Tenterden, which lies in the Weald, a certain right to claim him, but there are, of course a lot of other places in the Weald. More grounds are needed to justify the title of birth-place.

It is thought that Caxton was born around 1420. Parish Registers did not become compulsory until over 100 years later, but there are other documents that mention the names of ordinary people and places. By the fifteenth century even the bedel rolls were giving names to the workers and shopkeepers employed by the priory. Henry Luk, a carpenter, and his employees were building a new barn in Westwell in 1410 and were working in Appledore in 1415. (Could they have been the forebears who passed on their business acumen to the Lucks, the famous Kentish cider makers?) In the 1428 Appledore bedel roll there is a total of 14 names mentioned including that of one woman, Isabelle Baynold, who sold two pennyworth of lime. At this time Thomas Brykenden was renting the demesne farm and buying lime, tiles and timber from local suppliers and was employing local craftsmen as tilers and carpenters. John Myles, who was selling tiles then and again in 1433, was succeeded by Thomas Mylis in 1472 suggesting that this was an ongoing family business. And since man cannot live by timber and tiles alone, there must have been a host of other trades-people offering useful goods and services. It seems to have been a thriving community.

More importantly, there are many official documents still in existence, and as far as Caxton is concerned, more relevant ones. It appears that the Royal Commission on Historic Manuscripts, who initially suggested that Caxton might have been born in Tenterden, had been busy with various records of the corporations of Rye, New Romney and Lydd made in the fifteenth century. There were references to a John Cakstone and a William Causton (both phonetic spellings of Caxton, a usual practice at this time) in the Romney accounts prior to 1406. Later records refer to a lawyer, Thomas Kaxton of Tenterden who acted for Tenterden in disputes with Rye in the 1450s. In 1459 a Thomas Caxton became Common Clerk of Lydd, probably the same Thomas Kaxton as the one described as a lawyer. He held this office for some years and eventually became Bailiff of Lydd.

Clearly Thomas was a very able and highly respected man, and he forges a very strong link between the name Caxton and the town of Tenterden, but whether there was any link between Thomas Caxton and William Caxton is unknown.

Assuming William was born in 1420 he would have been in his thirties in the 1450s when Thomas Kaxton first comes to our notice. Discounting extreme longevity, which was not common at this period, it becomes likely that Thomas was quite a young man at this time, his age not very different from that of William. In this case, Thomas cannot have been William's father, but could have been a brother, cousin or even uncle. The probability of tracing any relationship is remote but it might be rewarding to look for clues.

William had been apprenticed to the Mercer's Company in London in 1438 and by the 1450s was probably living in Bruges (or Brugge) in Burgundy where he was employed in trading. At this time the import of cloth into Burgundy was subject to a lot of restrictions. Caxton proved rather good at finding ways round the law and as a result was able to help the Duchess of Burgundy with some business affairs in England. Both trade in English broadcloth and his own career showed a marked improvement after this. Appointed Governor of the English Merchants at Bruges in 1462 he was able to negotiate business arrangements for King Edward IV who, two years later, commissioned him as one of the ambassadors to the Duke of Burgundy. By 1468, when a commercial treaty was set up between the two countries, Charles the Bold had succeeded his father as Duke. He went on to marry Edward IV's sister, Margaret, and two years later Caxton entered her service as a commercial adviser and agent.

Margaret had a great knowledge and love of literature and it was under her influence that Caxton, who had already attempted to translate the *Histories of Troy* from French into English, was encouraged to complete the work. She also supported his passion for improving the English language, that 'brode and rude englishh' which he had picked up in the Weald. Altogether he translated some 21 books from French into English updating the language as he went. It seems that he never used one word when two would do – was this an artful device for enlarging the vocabulary of his reader? Perhaps, perhaps not - but Shakespeare and Milton and all the rest have a lot to thank Caxton for!

On a more practical note, the demand for Caxton's English translations became so great that he was driven to investigate the new art of printing. He set up his first printing press in Bruges in 1472, but by 1476 trouble was brewing between Burgundy and England, and so he returned to London and set up a printing press in Westminster.

The *Polychronicon* was the history of the world from its creation, which had been written by Ralph Higden, a monk of Chester, and translated into English by Trevisa. It was printed by Caxton who also wrote an introduction and a final chapter bringing the history up to the date of printing in the fifteenth century. A copy of this book was given to Tenterden by an American, Boies Penrose, in 1928. It remained stored away in the not-very-strong strong room in the Town Hall until its astronomic value made it necessary to give it stronger protection and also offer better facilities for its study, and it was moved to safer storage in Canterbury. The beautiful binding of the book is a modern replacement, but inside the print is as clear and the rag paper as white as it was on the day when Caxton himself saw it. It was easy to see why the invention of printing had such a dramatic and long-lasting effect. While important legal documents had been handwritten by the most skilful scribes, it took a good deal of head-scratching study to disentangle the handwriting – and meaning - of less able performers. With the advent of printing, each letter in every word was clear so that the text was easy to understand and reading – particularly when Caxton succeeded in replacing the archaic construction and long forgotten words of the early writings - became a pleasure.

Returning to the question of where William Caxton was born – the relationship between Thomas (certainly of Tenterden) and William is at least possible. Both were educated men who found employment in the world beyond their family confines and this in itself suggests that they had a similar background. Clearly both were talented men and clever when it came to dealing with the law, William's skill proving rather more rewarding than Thomas's! They were nevertheless both highly successful in their own fields and it seems that they earned their success by hard-work, honesty and – probably – thoroughly likable personalities. Thomas seems to have chosen the law for his career, while William chose – or was persuaded – that there was a good future in the Mercer's company. Perhaps this suggests that his family were not farmers/clothiers, for it is likely that he would have continued in that profitable lifestyle if that had been the case. It does appear more likely that he had an urban background and while Cranbrook and Goudhurst and Biddenden were places more strongly associated with cloth making than Tenterden, until more formal proof occurs, there is some justification for the theory that both Caxtons came from Tenterden.

Certainly as a proven fact it cannot be used. Since it is a theory based on secondary sources the possibility of fundamental errors is increased; it is so easy to misinterpret what someone else has written. However it can still be presented as a possibility – and until new evidence arrives to disprove or modify it - thoroughly enjoyed!

* * * * *

The Mystery of the Incompetent Carpenter

Opposite to the Town Hall in Tenterden High Street is the beautiful half-timbered house which is now called the Lemon Tree Restaurant. It is a largely unspoilt example of a Wealden Hall house built in the fifteenth century. There is, however, one feature which causes architectural historians considerable surprise: the clumsy carpentry of the middle part of the frontage. In the days when master carpenters were so very highly skilled, how did it come about that such a fine house was subject to such incompetent work?

The Lemon Tree Restaurant

This timber work is not part of the original building but took place when the house was modernised in the sixteenth century. Originally there was a central hall with projecting first floor chambers at both ends. The hall stretched up to a crown-post roof where smoke-blackened timbers testify to the fire which once burnt on a hearth in the middle of the floor. There was a parlour at the eastern side with a door into a lean-to pentice where stairs led up to the solar above which was provided with a garde-robe. Modern stairs have replaced the early ones but the way up into the solar is still the same as it always was. At the west end of the hall a cross passage ran from the front to the back door and on the far side of that there were three doors, the two central ones leading into the pantry and buttery, and the third one opening on to stairs leading to the chamber.

There was more grandeur than comfort in these halls with their draughts and smoke and lack of insulation. An inglenook hearth with a brick chimney, which not only kept the smoke under control but also made a huge storage heater, became a 'must-have' improvement and after the first introduction of this luxurious appointment modernising hall houses became extremely fashionable. While they were about it they built brick ovens for cooking and put in ceilings to retain the heat from the fire. This gave them extra space on the first floor. The upper room thus produced had its floor supported on girders and binders (timbers) which in turn carried the joists bearing the floor boards and usually the main girder was bedded into the new brick chimney at one end and supported on some timber framing at the other end.

The odd thing with this hall is that a ceiling was put in – but no hearth. However, there may be a reason. This house possessed something rather special – a detached kitchen. This kitchen was separately framed and set adjacent to the service rooms with its door close to the back door of the cross passage. It was open to the roof, and there was a loft constructed over half of the room on the end away from the fire which was built against a fireback on the south wall of the kitchen.

There was, therefore, no need for cooking facilities to be provided in the hall when the new ceiling was inserted but it still seems rather strange that that comfortable inglenook was not built.

Now it must have taken quite a long time to build a chimney for a lot of bricks were needed and you couldn't just phone the builder's merchant for supplies. They had to be made locally which, in itself, was a lengthy process. The ceiling could be put in much more quickly if the main girder was supported on timber posts. However, finding suitable trees in an area where a lot of them had been used for ship-building might have been difficult if not impossible.

Was that what happened here? The main girder supports the binders which carry the joists and in the centre of this girder is a slightly odd representation of a Tudor Rose. Is it possible that this was designed to celebrate Henry VIII's visit in 1538? The bailiff would have had advance notice of the visit for the progresses were planned long ahead of the event. Nevertheless producing bricks for a chimney would have been out of the question and finding the right bits of timber to support the girder, put in a ceiling and work out a way of making the place look like a modern continuous jetty house (like Smallhythe Place) can't have been easy. Poor old Bob the Builder must have done his best and 'got the job done' but it would not have been one that he was proud of and he probably complained about the problems for the rest of his life.

And did Henry ever see that Tudor Rose? As with Queen Elizabeth's arms painted in Harven, the house at Westwell, the carving does not prove that Henry visited the house. Maybe he did, maybe not – there were other dwellings in the town which might well have taken precedence when it came to receiving the king. On the other hand this hall was certainly in the middle of the town where a reception committee might have been expected to receive the royal party. Who knows? Sadly the records that might have told us what happened disappeared in the great fire and we are left to our own thoughts and imagination. At least, if we choose to accept this theory despite the fact that it is unproven, Bob can rest a little easier in his grave, exonerated by us from the charge of incompetence.

The Tudor Rose carved on the Girder in the Lemon Tree Restaurant

* * * * *

The Smallhythe Legend

The Smallhythe legend is a very different affair from the Westwell myth. It tells the romantic story of how that handsome and debonair prince, Henry VIII, came a-courting the lovely young Anne Boleyn in the flowery meadows and bosky lanes around her family farm (Bulleign Farm). And when, at the close of day Henry had escorted her back to the farm, he took himself off to his lodgings in – the undoubtedly rose-garlanded - Yew Tree Cottage. It does, of course, entirely neglect the fact that Anne was a sophisticated lady schooled in the courtly graces of the French Court before she met Henry, and that Smallhythe was one of the busiest industrial sites in England where even the most case-hardened blacksmith would have had second thoughts about taking his sweet heart for a romp in the hay. (It is uncertain whether Bulleign Farm was ever connected with Anne's family, but there is nothing to suggest that she ever visited this relatively humble dwelling.)

However, in 1538 Henry really did come to Tenterden. In the Tenterden Municipal Record Book there is an entry that says: *This yere ye XXVIII of Auguste King Henry VIII came to Tenterden.* There is nothing to say what he got up to when he was there but not a lot, one assumes, for it seems most likely that he used it merely as a stopping-off point on his way to Smallhythe. He probably knew more about Smallhythe than about Tenterden anyway, for although his galleon, the Great Harry was actually built at Woolwich around 1512, the timbers had been cut and prepared in Smallhythe. It was only because the Rother was becoming silted up and there was doubt about whether it was deep enough to float the great galleon downstream, that it was not constructed there. As it was, the carpenters walked from Smallhythe to Woolwich to complete the job.

By 1538 the French and Spanish had fallen out with Henry again. Now while his matrimonial attachments left much to be desired, his devotion to his kingdom and his efforts to defend it never faltered. He was aware that the French and Spanish liked nothing better than a bit of sacking and looting on the English coast but now a more serious invasion seemed imminent and so, this summer, he was making his annual progress around the south of England, checking on coastal defences and looking for ways to build up his navy. He must have needed to see for himself whether the erstwhile royal shipyard at Smallhythe was still capable of providing the vessels which he needed and it seems that this was so for the *Great Gallyon* and the *Lesse Galleon* were built after this visit - although the second ship may have been made nearby at Reading. This certainly seems to lend credence to the theory that Smallhythe was the intended destination of his journey.

Clearly he did not come to see Anne Boleyn for he had had her executed in 1536. Like some of us, the Bloggs family tend to be weak on dates.

The myth goes on to say that Henry stayed at Yew Tree Cottage. This is now a small brick cottage built probably around the beginning of the eighteenth century. Brick was the must-have building material at that time and with its big and impressive front door, now long gone, it would have been seen as a highly desirable residence. Moreover, although today we see ‘small’ as mean and poverty-stricken, in those days ‘small’ meant cosy and luxurious. No doubt the Joe Bloggs of the day would have considered that such an upmarket residence would have provided the most suitable place for the royal lodgings. The previous house on the site was a timber-framed building and there is no reason to think that it was architecturally memorable. In fact its rebuilding suggests that it may well have been inferior to Smallhythe Place. A recent comprehensive survey has revealed that this was originally a larger building and an impressive one, with grand oriel

Smallhythe Place

windows on the south and west sides. Moreover, the survey goes on to suggest that it was a public building and that the finest ground floor room could have been intended as a reception room for a person of rank. So perhaps it is more likely this was the building where the king was received.

There is one more indication that this might be the case. Ellen Terry, the Victorian super-star, bought the property in 1899. She loved old cottages and would not have them desecrated by the introduction of electricity or main water but she did make one concession for the benefit of James Usselman (who acted under the name of James Carew) her toyboy husband. As an American he didn't like her bucket loos at all and so she had the lamp room, a little extension which jutted out from the first floor, taken down and replaced with a smaller, state-of-the-art earth closet. This lamp room had a small window and was set in a secluded position at the back of the house so it is most unlikely that the term 'lamp room' means that it was an external lighting feature. It was probably just the room where Ellen stored her lamps. So what made her think of putting a new loo here?

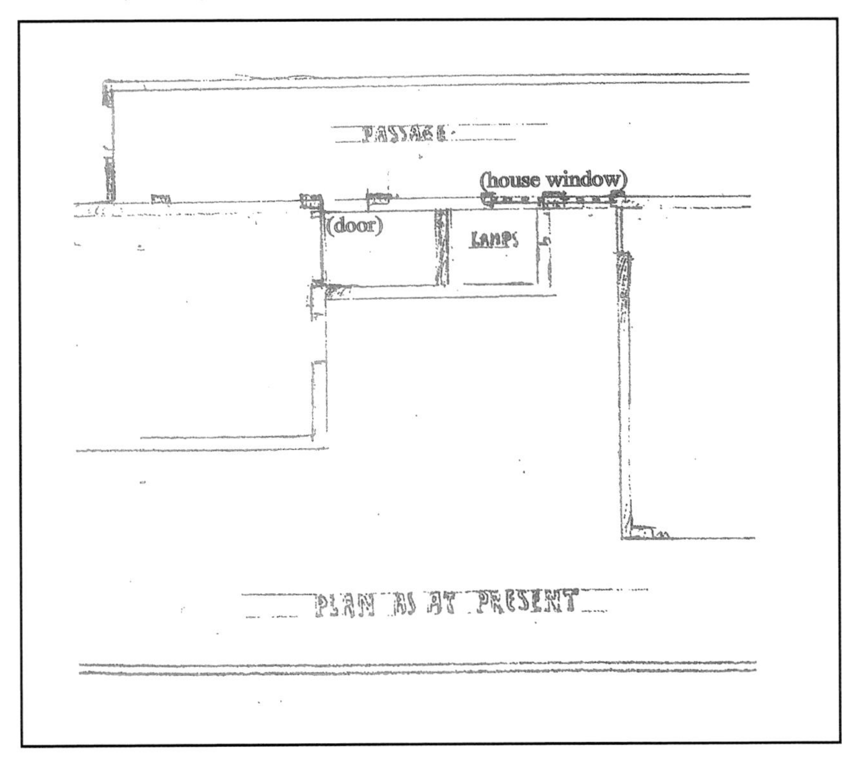

Builder's Sketch of the Lamp Room

The builders estimate and the plans for this extension, which include a sketch of the structure to be demolished, still exist. The construction details of the doorway leading into it show clearly that it was not put in when the house was first built so this 'lamp room' was a later addition. That explains why it stretched so far along the side of the house that it blocked out a window; you really cannot imagine that anyone would originally construct a window with a view of a store room (or lavatory!) The plan shows that the narrow little room was divided across the middle by something which is indicated by two lines with shading between them. This could not have been a door or wall so does it indicate a change in level?

In fact, small extensions jutting out of the first floors of early houses were usually privies and so that shaded division might indicate the presence of raised privy seat. Boarded over in some way, it would have made a shelf which Ellen would have been reluctant to use for the storage of anything more delicate than rather smelly oil lamps. Moreover, it is often the case that with medieval and very early houses there is something called 'continuance of usage' which means that over the years as houses are altered original features may be modernised but their use remains the same. Perhaps this is what happened here – it was an old garde-robe that gave Ellen the idea of replacing it with an up-to-date privy. (Later the earth closet was replaced by a WC which, although awkwardly and rather publicly situated at the top of a new stairway, was still in use until the end of the twentieth century.)

The original first floor garde-robe had been built in the end room and it was not common to have more than one in a house of this size. However, while Carew may have been fussy about his loos, Henry VIII was known to be obsessive about them and if he were coming to a public building he would almost certainly have demanded that a new lavatory should be built for his private use. So could this have been a garde-robe built especially for his visit? The royal progresses were planned so long in advance that there would certainly have been time for this to be done. It seems a likely explanation for such an odd little construction and, although of course this is only speculation, it could indicate that it was Smallhythe Place that welcomed the king.

And did he actually stay the night in Smallhythe, as the myth would have it? Long before the king and his household set off on their travels their hosts, living in the great houses of England, were warned of the horribly expensive honour to be inflicted upon them. Today there are still documents recording these journeys so we know that in 1538 the court moved from Eridge to Bedgebury and was there for the nights of 27 and 28 August. On 29 August it moved to Halden Park [now Halden Place] in Rolvenden, and on the next day travelled on to Ashford. So on 28 August we have Henry in Smallhythe, his household in Bedgebury and an anxious Sir John Dudley, with self-confessed cash flow problems, at Rolvenden awaiting the arrival of the court on 29 August.

The inspection of the river and discussions about the ships would surely, in view of Henry's love affair with his navy, have been dealt with at length. Then there was the question of meals which was, we assume, a major pre-occupation with the king. It is inconceivable that there was enough time left for him to ride back to Bedgebury on the twenty-eighth. So did he inflict himself and body guards on Sir John prior to the arrival of the main body of his henchmen – or did he stay in Smallhythe? It seems unlikely that he popped off anywhere else for a sleep-over. Shipwrights had equipped the vessels for the royal voyage to the Field of the Cloth of Gold and must have been quite capable of providing the comforts for a royal night's lodging. Sadly, there is absolutely no evidence to show where the king did spend the night so it is a case of: "You pays your money and you takes your choice!"

The old myth has spawned a new one. This tells a story of Henry's visit to Smallhythe accompanied by Anne Boleyn, of a fine banquet given in their honour and of a monk brought to the king in chains because of the seditious sermon he had preached. The king, in great good humour after so much feasting, pardons the monk and sets him free.

It seems that it was Ellen Terry who is to blame for this legend. For Ellen the 'Play was the Thing' and mere historical accuracy came a poor second to lively drama. So when a pageant was produced at Smallhythe the tale of the king's presence in the vicinity was given a dramatic fillip for the sake of good theatre – and lo and behold – another twist and turn was added to the Smallhythe Myth which, amidst all its spurious details, appears to retain the memory of one important fact – that Henry VIII once came to Smallhythe

* * * * *

The Mystery of why Tenterden got the date wrong.

Henry VIII's travels around the country with his enormous retinue are well documented in the *Itineraries* which still exist and record, not so much Henry's capers as those of his household. At least, they tell us where the party bedded down each night. It is from these documents that we learn that the king's household was in Bedgebury on the nights of 27 and 28 August 1538, and moved on to High Halden (Halden Park in Rolvenden) on 29 August. He could easily have ridden to Tenterden on 28 August 1538 – so why do local histories insist that it was in 1537?

Following a fire which destroyed most of Tenterden's records it could only have originated from the one surviving document, the Tenterden Municipal Record Book, and a transcript of this in Archaeologia Cantiana Volume 32 reads:

XXIX John Austen th' elder

[This yere ye XXVIII of Auguste Kinge Henry VIII came to Tenterden]

XXIX – the 29th year of the reign of Henry VIII – 1537! So why was that wrong? Eventually the reason became clear. It was due to that old trap – looking at the past as though it were the present.

In the sixteenth century there were no calendars to hang on the wall. The calendar itself, the Julian calendar, was not accurate, and dates were calculated by saints' days and the years of the king's reign. Tenterden, reasonably enough, went with the flow and dated events by whichever bailiff was in office.

The term 'this yere' did not refer to the calendar year, 1357 but to the bailiff's year of office, something which always began on 29 August. Thus John Austen, who was elected bailiff on 29 August 1537, was in office during September, October, November, December, January, February and March 1537 and since the calendar year began on 25 March, during April, May, June, July and until 29 August 1538. So the king's visit on 28 August occurred immediately before the end of John Austen's term of office and was in 1538.

Once you have assimilated the fact that the calendar year started on 25 March, the regnal year started on the date on which the monarch came to the throne, and the Tenterden year started on 29 August, it becomes possible to date events accurately and Tenterden's apparent errors in the dating of various national events disappear. A typical example concerns the Spanish Armada which was included in the events listed in the record book. This was in the time of Elizabeth I and the record reads:

XXIX Edward Gervis

[This yere the Spanyshe fleete came to Ingland about St James tide]

Since Elizabeth came to the throne in 1558, the twenty-ninth year of Queen Elizabeth's reign was 1586 – and so this suggests that the Record Book is dating the coming of the Armada to 1586.

However, Elizabeth came to the throne on 17 November 1558 so the twenty-ninth year of her reign ran from 17 November 1586 to November 1587. The term 'this yere' refers to Edward Gervis's year as bailiff, a position to which he was elected on 29 August. Clearly this cannot have been in 1586 but must have been on 29 August 1587 and so his term of office continued until his replacement in August 1588. St

James's day is 25 July and again this was towards the end of Gervis's 'yere' that is – in 1588 – which is the year in which the coming of the Armada actually took place. Maybe some of the good folk of Tenterden were finding this method of recording dates a bit cumbersome and 'old-fashioned' and so the bailiff decided to enter the calendar date as well! (The date 1588 is appended to the record of the Spanyshe visit.)

Some local reports are very interesting. A comet described as a '*blasing starr*' appeared in1577 (comet v1) and another (w1) in 1618, *'risinge towarde the East in the mornyng stremynge forwarde'*. In 1579 there was *'a gret earthquake the vi th day of Aprell about v or vi o clok at afternoon'*. Extreme weather occurred quite frequently over a period of ten years in the latter part of the seventeenth century. Following a *'great and fierce wind'* in February 1662 and another on 20 July of the same year, there was in 1671 a *'great flood and storm'* with *'Great Damage to the Nation by sea and land'* . In December 1672 Benenden steeple and church and 5 houses were burnt when struck by lightning, and in February 1673 another *great and fierce wind* blew down Staplehurst Spire and many barns.

One event of special local interest is the burning of Smallhythe which took place in the reign of Henry VIII:

VI Barthelemewe ffowle

[The which yere Smalide was burnte on the last day of Julye]

Barthelemewe was bailiff between 29 August 1514 and 29 August 1515, and therefore this *'last day of Julye'* occurred in **July 1515**.

What a blessing the Gregorian calendar is!

* * * * *

Final Thoughts

This has been essentially a search for the truth. Theory never professes to be an absolute truth but if the evidence on which the theory is based is good enough, it comes very close to it. Thus the theories that Horne's Place was, at least from the thirteenth century, the original site of the demesne farm and that its vicissitudes gave rise to the Appledore Myth can be accepted with few reservations.

Rather different is the story of the wandering chapel. It begins with an incontrovertible fact, namely that the chapel was dragged away to a new place, but thereafter the evidence becomes patchy. It would be wrong to say that this story is true but on the other hand, based as it is on pieces of sound evidence, it is not pure speculation or 'pie-in-the-sky'. Perhaps it is best to describe it as a truthful but out-of-focus snapshot in which details are hazy. It is not valueless because it can spark the imagination and lead to a search for clarification and further information.

The setting up of the new demesne farm and the development of the modern village of Westwell around it are beyond dispute. Equally certain is the fact that the early village lay some mile or two to the south of the existing village, but again much needs to be done to fill in details and complete the story. With most myths and mysteries this is the case.

Some legends such as that of the Demon Archer or Caxton's birthplace do not lend themselves to a search for evidence through primary sources such as medieval balance sheets or the built environment. At the best they do no more than hint at some kind of truth to be understood only with imaginative perception.

As Pontius Pilate said, "What is truth?" For us, maybe, no more than our ultimate aspiration.

APPENDIX

Appledore

Black Pudding stones remaining in the undisturbed stonework and the top of the arch over the undercroft doorway. The square socket may have held a beam to support the original joists for the floor above the arch. A small 13th century column once flanked the door in the west wall.

The west wall of the chapel.

The undercroft door

Westwell

The artificially levelled platform with the track from the old Rectory on the right-hand side and Parsonage Farm house set on the left edge, the front of the house rising from the ground at a lower level. Was this because the first part of the 16th century house was built as an extension to an existing building?

Prior Eastry's Mill (rebuilt)

Queen Elizabeth's Arms in Harven

Tenterden

The Polychronicon

The binding is new but the first page is part of the book actually printed by William Caxton.

Bibliography

John Tosh	*The Pursuit of History (2000)*
R.A.L, Smith	*Canterbury Cathedral Priory (1969)*
C.R. Haines	*Dover Priory*
John Newman (Pevsner)	*West Kent and the Weald (1980)*
John Newman (Pevsner)	*North East and East Kent (1969)*
Sir John Winnifrith	*History of Appledore (1983)*
Hugh Roberts and Gordon Herd	*Caxton – Man of the Weald (1976)*
S. Sweetinburgh	*Territorial Organisation of the Church An Historical Atlas of Kent (2004)*
Jill Edison	*Romney Marsh, Survival on a Frontier (2000)*
Cecil Hewett	*English Historic Carpentry (2001)*
R. W. Brunskill	*Timber Building in Britain (1985)*
R.W. Brunskill	*Brick Building in Britain (1997)*

R.W.Brunskill — *Houses and Cottages of Britain (2000)*

RCHME — *A Gazetteer of Medieval Houses in Kent (1994)*

E.Hasted — *The History and Topographical Survey of the County of Kent VII (1798)*

Hugh Roberts — *Tenterden, the First Thousand Years*

David Hey — *The Oxford Companion to Local and Family History (2000)*

Elizabeth Hollis — *The Westwell Chronicles (2008)*

Archaeologia Cantiana

A.H.Taylor — *Municipal Records of Tenterden Vol XXXII (1917)*

Gordon Ward — *Saxon Records of Tenterden Vol XLIX (1938)*

Mary Adams — *History of the Demesne Farm at Appledore. Vol CXII (1993)*

Mary Adams — *Development of Roof-tiling and Tile-making on some mid- Kent Manors Vol. CXV (1996)*

John F. Potter — *Anglo-Saxon Roofing Techniques Vol CXXVI (2006)*

Mary Adams — *Westwell, the Establishment of a Village Vol CXXVII (2007)*

Other Sources

Photo-copy of Prior Eastry's Memorandum Book

Leases and Wills and sundry other records held at Hall House, Appledore in the care of the National Trust

Also in my possession:

'The Medieval Moated Site at Parsonage Farm, Westwell, Kent. First Draft', CTRL Integrated Site Report Series, Jan 2006 J. Hill

Who Killed the British Earthquake? R.M. Wood & C.Melville

Council of Valdés Municipal Archives

Sundry transcripts form bedel rolls of Appledore, Westwell, Great Chart, Hollingbourne.

Information from the Henry VIII Itineraries regarding the King's progress through Kent in 1538, and from *Letters and Papers* regarding his visit to Sir John Dudley at Halden Park in the same year. Supplied by Dr Starkey

* * * * *